Keyhole Hero

Keyhole Hero

by

Cassandra Lee Wiltz

Published by:

Oak of Acadiana Publications
18896 Greenwell Springs Road
Greenwell Springs, LA 70739

ISBN 978-1-950398-69-0

Printed in the U.S., the U.K., Australia and the U.A.E.
For Worldwide Distribution

Dedication

I would like to dedicate this book to my mom, my hero.

You are the **wHOLEkey!**

Acknowledgments

4 plus 1

Grace

To my father: thank you; if you had not abused my mother,

we could not see how much strength of God was within her

for all of our betterment, including you.

Thanks for admitting to me how much of God she had inside.

Thanks for confessing to me before your death.

Thank you for what seemed to be only 5 hours of normalcy,

moments I have seen you in your beautiful best state.

Thank you for being the seed I needed you to be,

the seed that produced me, **Cassandra Lee**.

Thanks for being my dad.

I want to acknowledge my spiritual mother,
Andrea McDougal,

our

Queen of Victorious High Teas.

You have reminded me endlessly who I am and suggested I write a book years ago.

I can never repay you for all you have poured into me in such a short time.

Your tenderness and guidance are a haven for fractured hearts.

You heal us with your love and genuineness. I will forever be indebted to you.

You have an exceptionally special etch in my heart. **Thank you**.

Special thanks to **God**, my **Heavenly Father**, my **family**, and **all** who encouraged me to write.

Thank you for your heartfelt urges and motivating tactics to ensure my journey as an author manifested.

I am grateful to have every one of you in my life.

Contents

Hero History Holes

Preface

This book is about happenings from my childhood. Everything you read in this story is actual events. After reading my mom's truth optimistically, I pray the reader would receive light or more insight into my perception.

⚷ Helping heroes thought:

Ending each **hole** (chapter) are my thoughts memoed.

⚷ Helping heroes introspection:

I have added my meditative concept for every topic.

⚷ You are Covenant-created:

With scripture, each opening helped me to reflect on and add hope. **The Word** has promises for our life, when we are faced with unutterable occurrences in reality.

⊶🔑 Hole 1:
The Walk

Don't ask me, Cassandra; answer when they ask you what your dad did.

My mom stands on the other side of the glass with a blank stare. A lady named Paula Smith helped me. I am sitting on the floor now, ready to describe.

How did I get here? Where am I? I'm glad you asked. My keyhole hero and I just walked from home to the Police station. **Mom is upset and is firm.** She said she needed me to tell them all he did. I will not say one thing to anyone; Momma, my "keyhole hero," will die if I answer something. His direction is embedded within. I have already made up my mind.
She doesn't know it yet.

Let me tell you; I made a deal with the devil, well, not actually; in my case, it was my father.
Or was he?

Maybe he's not the devil, or perhaps he's the devil's son.

These are my real thoughts, honestly. I meditated on it as a teen-ager, still trying to understand it years later. Sometimes I actually thought it wasn't him, but what do I know?

Tales my father told me. It was a promise made to my father. I would not **confess** one word, or my hero would die, which would be my fault.

My mother seemed to look through me as Ms. Paula used such skill, understanding my struggle. She brought out these stuffed dolls. It was challenging for me to communicate. But through the toy dollies, I could show instead of speak.

The daddy and Cassandra dolls were in my hand, each fully dressed. I pretended it was a puppet show, like Fridays in kindergarten. I demonstrated each touch as she asked me questions without say-ing one word. I tucked away memories of what my father did to me. As I sat there, I remember thinking this thought all day while he did whatever he could without causing me to scream out.

This deal became concrete. Solid, I became in keeping my word of promise. Now I became controlled, silent.

A covered mouth beyond 21 days, it works, a habit-forming. I de-cided I would help Momma from getting hurt.

The Walk

All harm happened in the last room on the left. Straight down the hall, same space of torments, both of us.

Abused constantly, I never thought I would be like our mom.
I always prayed to be just like her. My prayer was answered, And as crazy as it may sound, I'm thankful. **She endured more than I ever did.**

My mother was disgraced everywhere in our house, outside of it too. Somehow seeing it through the keyhole, his violence seemed worse—as he hurt my hero daily, it seemed, unless he wasn't home.

From my experiences inside the evil chamber, I knew I'd die from being so scared at times. On countless occasions I felt like death was standing, waiting to collect me.
Was it?

I always felt something was there, often wondering without pondering further.
As I think of it, my life was threatened several times in this area. But not by this particular molester, with another.
That's another piece; stay tuned. I will tell you more about it, maybe in the following script.

At this time, helping my protector is the main feature.

⊶—⚓ Helping heroes thought:

Be careful as you pray.
Ask with a clear understanding of your request.
Covet to be like yourself more than anyone else.

⊶—⚓ Helping heroes introspection:

Do you want an invitation to receive a person's pain? Consider this next time you desire to be identical to another or say, I want to be just like you. Please be cautious. Envision experiencing discomfort when the prayer is answered. Be precise if you have no intention of accepting extra warfare meant for the One you wish to be.
Is this coincidence, or was this purpose?

⊶—⚓ You are covenant-created

:Yet my unfailing love for you will not be shaken, nor my covenant of peace be removed, says the Lord, who has compassion on you.

Isaiah 54:10b

HOLE 2:

Returned Home

I remember it like it was yesterday. My mom came home from work that day. I ran to meet her when a friend dropped her off and gave her a ride home. Outside now, I hugged my mom.

I was so happy to see her. My father didn't want me to go outdoors with her, but I didn't obey him. I ran out of the house against the orders he gave me. He said, "Don't you go outside, Cassandra. Sit here by Daddy until your momma comes inside the house … if she can stop running her mouth to that fool out there." **I said no and ran out.**

I wanted to be with my mom all the time. Once I held her waist, I was excited and felt safe near her. I felt loved with an unexplainable warmth in her presence.

I heard her colleague say, "Is it okay if I get down for a little while?" My mom said, "No, I have to cook and clean for the kids; I'll talk tomorrow." The lady, a Caucasian friend named Ms. Donna, loved my mom. Somehow I know she knew my mom suffered and was in danger. My mom tried to make Ms. Donna leave, but she lingered, speaking of work. She tried hard, trying to get my mom to laugh. I saw this in less than 5 minutes of their goodbye visit. My hero a look stoic, staring and seeing, I believe, what was waiting for her inside.

Finally, my mom said, "Look, thank you for the ride, but I've got to go." I became so nervous and hugged my mom much tighter at that moment. I knew what waited for her inside. My stern mom said, "Now, I will see you tomorrow," knowing the longer she stayed out, the madder this violent person would become.

I looked up at my mom because I knew that reaction, rushing someone to leave; mom's face showed her to be a thousand miles away. She was getting rude and seemed not to care because the longer she took by Ms. Donna's car, the angrier he would be in his reason for it being all her fault. He said this every time he hit my mom. He was supposed to pick her up this day, Friday payday. He'd already collected her paycheck for her lunch break. We all know the routine. He's home early and light-headed. I say that nicely, for now at least.

Once she walked through the door, my dad would grab my mother without letting her sit down after a long workday. Even at a young age, I knew and understood more than I could express. Knowing what's next became very typical for us. I wished mom would take off with Ms. Donna, but I didn't want to leave my siblings alone with him either.

"Now, look what she did," my dad spoke to himself right before it was the time we expected her home. This statement was said whenever she had to catch a ride from working as a seamstress at Martin Mills, a factory. She labored very hard there. I know because I always hear her friends say it when I am in their company.

Her dream was to become an evangelist. She later decided to work private duty as a CNA and took compassionate care of every single patient in her care. I recall because I went with her on several occasions when she did Home Health.

My mom was genuine, distinctly to each need of every single patient. As I think about it, I realize this was part of her purpose and gift. She loved each one like she was their daughter and they (man/woman) were her birth parents. She was the most integral worker, and still to this day, I deeply admire the work ethic I received from her.

As we were under her supervision, the woman of **supernatural** strength never thought of herself as a helpless victim or pitied her years of disgrace and humiliation from her most complex patient ever, my father.

Carroll Antoine Wiltz, Sr., son of Adam "Harry" and Marie "Mayah" **nee Jones** Wiltz; he is the man I feared as my siblings did too. Her most challenging assignment as a breadwinner was remaining a punching bag for whatever he chose to accuse her of doing. When his ruthless clone decided to show present to her and us as she returned home from a hard day, it was even more complicated once she stepped into the house of hell with my dad's demons.

My father was beautiful by portrait and seemed to be decent through his disguised look as a man. His mind was intelligent; in reality, he was, but with a Hyde twist only seen behind a hole I often looked through or worse at any time, or anywhere in the home, an attack of his maniacal could strike her without notice. At least she knew savage behavior would happen once he dragged her to the room or continued asking her to go in there.

My dad's silent internal **rages,** taken out on my mother, had cycles. We learned how he operated, so we usually knew what he'd do next. I am not sure which one was worse for her, nor have I asked her from my curiosity. Through all of his death-dealing attempts, she remained one of the most balanced individuals and the strongest woman I will ever know. In my sight, no one will ever show as intensest as my hero seen through the keyhole.

⚷━ Helping heroes thought:

Be grateful for times of peace without disruption and relief from a long workday, and don't take these moments for granted. As my mother didn't get many days of it when living with an alcoholic and abusive spouse/partner, I'm sure countless others with similar life situations have too many days without rest. May you be sealed in His eternal peace.

⚷━ Helping heroes introspection:

Do you get the opportunity to unwind and count your blessings after a long stressful day without someone fist fighting you as soon as you open your door to the place called home, which is supposed to be where the heart is?

How much "worse" would you allow your spouse or significant other to do to you before saying I can't keep this promise when you vowed in marriage? Are ten years of it enough? Or do we stay with violent partners regardless of how much they belittle us and show no value of our worth?

⚷━ You are covenant-created

For thus saith the Lord GOD, the Holy One of Israel; In returning and rest shall ye be saved;

in quietness and in confidence shall be your
strength: and ye would not.   Isaiah 30:15

The Keyhole

Right below the knob, which was round, it held the keyhole used to look or lock the door so that no one could open it. My Dad preferred it closed. He always locked it like that would hide the demonic entity operating behind the scenes. He had a terrible **allegiance** to Satan, the enemy of every man and child; in this case, this enemy showed the hatred he felt and convinced my dad to learn of the evil way of doing things to and through a human being.

My siblings saw merciless actions and me not only through the keyhole, unfortunately. My dad was doing these things to his wife, my mom.

Like behind a closed door isn't humiliating enough, he sometimes did it outdoors. Through his own words, he told me himself-she was a wonderful woman, and he loved her **(so he thought)**; signing his name on the devil's line showed him as one having contempt toward her. Did he even know what love of the one you've pledged covenant with until eternity for better meant? Did he intentionally marry her, knowing he'd inflicted lethal as a weapon to see if she'd keep her vow, and he is shown as 95% worse? Did my mom ever experience love from the one she said, "I do?"

Questions I still have. Don't think I didn't inquire because many times I tried to pry answers from her, but until this very day, she has not spoken a single lousy word of her twice-married mortal.

During my dad's temperament fits or flares, we complained enough that after his frenzy was over, the hard-hearted one would leave her for dead every time. Deadly seconds of our more than a conquer victor were observed as he instructed us to watch, don't move, and stop that crying. Hate was beginning to brew within for this monster of a dad. Without words, through actions only, he gave his worst daily, sometimes as his way of saying, "Bertha, **I love you this much.**"

I grew up saying, "I'm never getting married." From my darkest years, I noticed it wasn't a happy connection or type of situation any child should experience. He showed it so many days by saying, "I will beat you to death if you don't do what I say," was a repeated saying of my father. He trained us to be stilled through his fatal language expressed to her.

We understood you don't talk back; his **out-of-control** echoed with a slap or a punch. We learned to expect my dad's turbulence without warning. He seemed to enjoy the image of a losing opponent's eyes sealed closed by hitting her somewhat like in a twelve-round boxing match, but my mother never defied him, and my mom endured more rounds than 12. It was no contest. If he didn't get tired, it would go on all night—a fight with only one keeping count and the other not throwing one hit back to defend herself or win one round. He viciously and sarcastically would say, "I'm going to seal them tonight; you just watch and see."

I assume he continued because he wanted his children to cheer on his actions. We were couch potatoes as he dared us to move with tears streaming down our faces. Now that I think of my mother and what an incredible strength she possessed most times, she'd tell us "It's okay" during his rampaging. Momma reassuring us disturbed the savage in him; her saying it increased his brutality.

Back to my mother's unimaginable restraint, it's easy to fight back. Now that I see it, she was more powerful than him. It's harder to restrict oneself. As I said, he counted how many times he hit her per night and told her she wanted him to do this. The bullying line we all memorized is: "You want me to do this." That's when we knew a destructive entity had come to visit.

If I screamed during a beating, he said, "Well, tell your momma to stop; can't you see what she's making me do?" He would even say, "I'm not doing anything!" And he was. His stormy voice would howl, "Tell your momma to stop!"

Can you imagine? My mom did nothing that our eyes saw but work, come home with a ride if he didn't pick her up, if she felt her death through a friend extending kindness offering her a ride home, she'd reject the offer. She'd choose to walk home. Walking must have been exhausting from a long day. To meet the production goal expected from her employer at the warehouse employing her at the time included repetitious movement. Our house of horrors was miles away.

Every unit had a lady or man overseeing the seamstress as they sewed, exerting themselves to make T-shirts and underwear for Fruit of the Loom. The individual is a floorwalker. In the factory, every type of seamstress section's goal was to complete the make of the shirt or undergarment by the set production amount given to meet the quota.

My mom hustled going in early, staying late, all this effort to be picked up by Dad on check day, to have her paycheck gone before the night was over. I remember my mom saying my dad would go into her job and make a scene, embarrass her, beat her in front of co-workers, and humiliate himself by trying to degrade her with his brute force, as he often did. Who can continue with this type of environment? **A cycle**.

Overtime pay ... she worked it to purchase and pay the bills due. Extra money was for our school supplies, whatever our education required to complete each grade. Every subject with no exception, regardless of what we saw at home or, for me, behind the keyhole, our duty was to bring home all A's. We could expect a whipping if we dared to bring home a C.

The Keyhole

We received finger swaps, and if sass reported for the conduct, it was her leather belt named **Bertha Butt.** That belt was not dead; it was alive and had feet to walk and hands to do the work she instructed it to do as the lash ran across our buttocks or landed anywhere on us as she swung.

They were a team. Bertha Butt, the belt, was mom's alter ego. My mom didn't talk, but baby Bertha Butt indeed did, and no one wanted to have a conversation with Ms. Leather. She always hung on her hanger. It looked like she was the commander of the closet. The clothing and other things inside were very organized, everything my mom treasured.

As I think of it, Keyhole Hero insisted we always keep it spotless. And yes, she assured us we were to see her inspect the entire house like clockwork, ensuring we stayed consistent with chores and not be idle one moment. She and my grandmother had a saying, "Idleness is the devils' playground." On her knees, she checked under the beds for trash. One piece out of order, and we knew what was next; never a shock, we attempted to duck from what seemed like an electric voltage from her hands with lightning speed and the bolt holding fire others see in the sky through bad weather. Still, this yellow color our eyes saw as our senses felt a severe sting sent to remind our mind of the lingering pain or bruise, branded now from not cleaning properly.

How could she keep this type of balance? While enduring, I still ponder her exceptionality; she always said we all have a cross to bear. As I recollect, I now see she carried a similarity to the old wooden cross we couldn't see at the time. She trusted God.

She was an unchanging, without an excuse yet abused mother, **never** complaining or saying a negative word about my Dad in the pitch-black darkest night perception. I saw nothing without **His light** from her example.

I want to tell you of our house's dark rooms game as we played with all we experienced —towels or blankets covering all windows and walking through our home in lightless rooms all had a tint darker than a car classified as illegal. A hell of a bad ... I mean sometimes felt like the worse set of cards we now were holding. Carroll Jr., significantly, I think, could feel more from this horrific deck dealt because of being a boy, feeling more like a protector, like the night he fought my dad. You'll read more of it in another book all about him.

Unable to see clearly or how it would affect us in his vicious moments, he kept us caged. He created an experience in which to encounter like the night we are all up, my father harming my hero until the clock rings. **It's my mom's alarm.** His chaos and confusion lasted all night; it was now morning; we didn't sleep. The answer would be no reader if you asked, "Did the violent parent stop the noise after the buzzer warned of the time?" Instead, he broke the clanging alarm clock from ringing in his ear. He said he purposely wanted us to hear him bring to pass and eventually destroy my mom while we hoped and prayed it would be impossible. He had to be boisterous at home during his blackjack game. Supernaturally from this seemingly endless wicked night, she is still alive.

Did he see value in our faces during this game which felt like 21 hours long? Reader, he was blinded by evil. **I believe God heard us.**
Tired, weary, broken, and bruised would not stop this unknown alien from dotting her eyes as he called it, "I'm going to close them; keep playing with me, Bertha," repeated words said by my father, ending with "you are going to see." She often couldn't see after a fight with him, nor was it sarcasm. **So, why did he say it?**

That must have been some psychological trick the enemy would play on my father because the unseen force knew my mother was given a gift from Heaven to see **(a seer).** She predicted the death of her father before the age of 18, devastating her once it came to pass. I believe that is why he tried to blind her by always focusing intently on closing her eyes during his madness. I call her an old wise owl sitting and seeing in and through the most challenging darkness of so many awful nights. She sat on her branch wherever she could rest for the moment. Until an unilluminated creature, or whatever the worst imagined villain your mind can fathom, pretended to be my male parent; he would disturb her externally with brutal physicality, but he failed from trying to steal her God-given peace held internally.

Throughout her life, as I recognize, it had to be God, the Creator of all life, living inside and keeping her alive. Behind the keyhole, her encounters with someone similar to a grim reaper turned rapist doing disgusting indefinables which seemed near death more often than not, as I took in my mother's scourge with Mr. Hyde.

Traumatic was my view of crucifying persecution through the hole, the room he used for his wretchedness and maltreatment. We beheld his sharpest countless instances marking us in his favorite place, the home's heart. Was he indicating he was heartless to us? Was he illustrating his heartbreak in the kitchen without saying a word? The place he showed himself most forceful. There's an old saying that the way to a man's heart is through cooking. Why didn't it work for my father? My mother cooked every day; why wasn't it enough? She was a great cook, and her biscuits made from scratch were our favorite.

Corruptly, the **doppelgänger** we called dad repeatedly displayed his cruelty to our torchbearer; all of us perceived her woes.

In my opinion, his favorite threatening object used a real butcher knife. It was huge. I had never seen anything like it. My mom didn't even use it to cut a single thing in that kitchen. And yes, our protector was cut before our eyes like it was a standard way of receiving our daily bread. Sometimes it appeared my father's barbaric sliced like a loaf; it depended on which sadist showed up for the day or night of horrors. He would slice himself too. If and when it happened, he'd shout, "Look at what you made me do!" And, yep, Mom was beaten for each cut he got too. Some say a child or woman should never experience it. **We did**.

⚷══ Helping heroes thought:

How are the real evil games of life distributed to us?
Who selects the runner representing the nation,
for a people to overcome the worse suffering and
death-like inflictions?
Should our minds inquire about the matters bleed-
ing in our hearts,
or should we understand the worst persecutions
happen to all who follow Christ?

⚷══ Helping heroes introspection:

Do we believe God lives within us?
After all of these shared memories, can you say
you'd still believe?
I believe my mother is proof, with an unmovable
faith, that He does.
Consider whom you would choose to fight to the
death in your region or among your immediate
family members.
The truth is, I would scream and volunteer, shouting,
"my mom," as the Capital inquired of our division.
Peeping through the keyhole, I would guarantee
my mom as our prizewinner after all my eyes saw.
She is my hero.

I can honestly say I would choose us again for every
excruciating obstacle. Since we are living proof to

be over-comers, I am affirmed we'd have victory for the team win.

Do you believe we agree to our sufferings on Earth before we arrive or are birthed into life?

Are we equipped as a champion at birth?

I would say the answer is yes. Would you?

Realize you are the chosen patron for your purposed feat.

Please repeat after me: I am triumphant against my worst enemy.

Know without a doubt, hero; you are born for this.

If my mother had a declaration, it should say:

Bertha Lee, chosen to bear fatal bandages, at liberty she,

remained loyal in 10 years of brutal and murderous treatment.

I believe the witnessing heavens will trumpet this for her day of judgment.

What will heaven announce for your accounts?

⌇⟶ You are covenant-created

Truly I say to you, whatever you bind on earth will be bound in heaven, and whatever you loose on earth will be loosed in heaven.

Matthew 18:18

The Lighter - The Devil in Disguise

I heard momma whimpering and whispering, "Carroll, stop, please stop." I heard momma speak in her voice filled with unspoken hurt from my male parent's torture from his past and present demons. I listened to my daddy say, "Shh!" to hush momma's mouth standing on the other side of the closed door.

Behind the keyhole, my eye saw through the opening big enough that Momma was naked on the bed. Daddy made her lie down. I saw a semblance like my father standing over Momma, and I heard the **flicker**, with his hand between her legs. Was he burning her with the fire from the lighter? Was he trying to start a fire like someone about to match charcoal on a grill?

Did I hear Momma say, "Ouch, Carroll, ouch?" I reminisced about wanting to help my mother as I lost focus scanning the room. Completely covered are the windows. I remember blinking uncontrollably. Not only foiled, but also when Dad was mad, he set on dark blankets over the thick curtains so no one could see into the outside glass. He did not want the neighbors to see him intently harming her.

I wanted to help my momma, but I did not know how. The least I could do was stand there and pray he didn't kill her.

I stared at all the things he did to her. I watched my hero, protector, and everything suffer for many days. On this date, all siblings were outside because he sent us there, but I dwelled with Mom. I hid in her closet instead of listening to his instructions. I did not want to leave her alone with him. I would see in her eyes the fear of the animal about to show up in the room.

When he told us to go outside until he called us back in, I did not listen. I crouched inside to see if I could help my mom. Momma's voice skipped; she was holding back her cry. I heard this as I walked silently from the closet to the door's keyhole.

I heard her ask, "Why are you doing this? I did not do anything! Please stop!" but he did not. I eavesdropped to a fit of unfamiliar anger; it sounded wicked, like an ugly answer from a creature of the wild, a beast that devours humans and animals from made-up or make-believe stories, movies we watched on a television screen. It had to be, wait, but this was real. I think back to stilling myself, so he would not know I was close to the door. I held my breath in my mind, so he could not hear me breathe or make a noise.

I was watching him hurt my mom. The one I felt so safe with, she made us pray every night.

I had moved back with my mom and siblings.
Before then, I was strengthened and reared by my grandmother Virven "Vivian" **nom de jeune fille** Louis, Mason.

Daily at 5 pm I deeply longed for my mom, and I missed her like I could not live without her. The hour mentioned was the time her shift at work ended. She would visit me on the weekends, but it was like I was so empty all week. Although I loved my grandmother, I was always so grieved within. Now that I reflect, it was the pain they were enduring that my spirit was in **sync**.

Prayer was a must, and we never missed a day praying. My mom was the only one who cooked and worked so hard every day. **Why is this happening to her?** Why was she chosen to bear such abuse?

Tears began to fall from my inability to make a sound to let her know I was right here with her through her torment and pain from the outer darkness. I was with her through degradation or similar to an African **castration**, but this was with fire. He was burning her with a cigarette lighter. He didn't smoke, but he'd light one up, take a puff and burn her with the cigarettes she smoked. I heard Mama cry silently yet loud, watching her tears sound through each fallen stream; it was like awaiting a long drop into a deep well. A fountain filled with all of her tears. No one knew Mama had a well filled with tears from my father's insane torture just because he thought she deserved to be treated worse than a dying animal from all the abuse, which led to the deliberate and calculated physical betrayal.

Mama said, "Ouch, you are hurting me, Carroll! Please don't do this. Carroll, please! What did I do?" Again, the dirty voice, which seemed like a boogeyman, we, as children or adults, sometimes tell tall tales to bring laughter, in this case, fear to entertain the audience. Her story was revealed behind the keyhole; I saw it all. I don't forget getting dizzy and desiring to be invisible and invincible, so he would not know I was there or harm me if he found out I was.

My Dad was flickering and holding the lighter now I see the fire burning my mom. Her cry has turned up mom's sound of the words she tried to release during this time of private parts set on fire like lighting a wick on a candle.

What I saw became severely blurry from welled-up tears and my water-filled eyes. I began conditioning a stillness of myself at such an early age.

I had a back-and-forth rock. I did it several times a day. I'm unsure how I could control my nervousness in those moments, which seemed like eternal years never to end of my mother not understanding what she had done to upset and cause this.

It was nothing she'd done. My mom was extremely quiet. She was a hard worker and didn't speak much; she sometimes worked to get her paycheck taken from her by my Dad. He'd drink the money away and not pay one bill. If he got a job, which he so luckily did on numerous occasions, he'd drink his paycheck away too.

My mom was **humiliated** behind the keyhole, but publicly with blackened eyelids, and a makeup artist did not cause this. She'd have to go and ask for extensions, praying this time, she could pay the bills like she promised those who lent her the money or gave her the loan.

She spoke so much as I remember my mother's eyes without saying one word. At five years old, yes, I can say I fully understood. She talked to me as I stared and looked, without a word said.

Then, when I could see her thoughts, she'd say, "Stop looking at me! Find something to do! Get out of my face!" She didn't want me to know the anguish within; she kept it hidden. My mom refused to allow us to carry a burden or give her pity. If you looked at her as a stranger not understanding each other's soul language, you might say she was cold and careless. Her statement of getting out of my face spoken to me was because I could now see and get the stories she never shared, complained about, or protested. That's right. How she did it boggles me; it was the strength of God. He made her solid rock-like to carry and continue with Carroll, who deliberately inflicted demonic, perverted threats and attempts of her death. Yes, he **coerced** killing her every time he drank the poison.

Nothing was **incredible** about my dad's revealing of his uncontrolled **hulk**.

Was it my dad speaking like some killer possessed by demons? It looked like him; as I stared, I came to see; I wiped my right eye and looked with my left.

I need to go in. I remember thinking, I need to know if it's him. It appears to be him from the back. It seems like he is standing there from his built, short, medium-sized structure. I hear my mom's throat hiccup from being choked and attempting to whisper, but a Bic lighter is burning her, and my father is holding the flick and her neck, yet he was not part of any circus act.

It was his weapon of choice in this instance of tormenting my mother. My mother asked my dad if he was crazy when he showed her the lighter. **This infuriated him.** He burned her until she went numb because she tried to stop him as the first fire flicked, but then she didn't fight anymore; tears streamed down her face. I was crying too, while I peeped through the keyhole.

My father (if it was him) said, "If you move your hand again, I will break it." He inhaled her pain like a hooked cokehead snorting the line straight off the table. Whatever this being was, it loathed some of the deadliest pain on my hero.

"Carroll, don't please," said Mom as this constricting to her neck was like a chaser after his drug of choice through this incident (was it) or an abusive training session of my father silencing my mom, who believed in God. She called on God in that minute, or was it longer?

She said, "Please!" My father is speaking like something from another dimension, from a planet with the ugliest creatures ever made. Nowhere near Earth is how I, **Cassandra Lee** see it as an adult.

Now I understood why. It couldn't be my father, the one of which we were terrified. He'd placed fear in my other siblings once I joined them in witnessing this. It wasn't until he was imprisoned, not from the torture he did to her, for abusing me, one year only, that I realized how many phobias from his pitilessness impacted me. What a great system of justice we have! **To serve and protect**—I will speak about this in another book in the future.

He threatened her during this mad moment as He said she made him do it. He stated at that moment he would hurt the kids if she didn't get this nasty burn. She said, "No, Carroll! No!" If she was too loud, a slap to her face out of nowhere, I wonder how she found the strength to speak out for her kids during her bonfire moments, similar to our high school at homecomings or jamborees.

Even through this callous moment, she mothered us as if it had never happened. As I look back and write these pages, I realize what an incredible mother I have in her. **My champion indeed.**

⚡ Helping heroes thought:

To suffer with Him means to reign with Him.

I'm not saying you should suffer and get mistreated on purpose.

I am simply reminding you that this is a promise when you feel comparable about going through a living hell in your darkest hour.

Remember Christ on the Cross for you to get you through.

⚡ Helping heroes introspection:

What Superhero antic has God placed within you to prove you bear His divine essence in torturous moments as my mother experienced?

Do you want to get a crown in Revelation?

You are purposed to go through hell on Earth moment(s) to show the world and others that you are more than a conqueror(s).

⚡ You are Covenant-created

And do not fear those who kill the body but cannot kill the soul. Rather fear him who can destroy both soul and body in hell.

Matthew 10:28

⚷—🔑 HOLE 5:

The Dog Doesn't Dance

Surprise, Daddy bought a pet. He just walked through the door with a pup.

Did you guess?

It's a puppy; finally tonight may not be a fight. We are all excited. I can see my father has been drinking, and something is wrong. After repeating this destructive cycle of how the room feels, even though we ignore it, we all understand that something wicked is in the room.

At this time, we are all gathered in the living room. We pass the shaking little dog around, out of one set of hands, then to another; we are super excited for a doggie. We are joyous but only for a moment.

He seemed to be a sweet pooch. The little dog was so scared that his shivering was noticeable. If I haven't shared it yet, my dad is an alcoholic. He is amusing and seems to be a great guy when sober. We, especially me, saw not many days of this side of him.

This particular night would be considered a "Pet Cemetery" scene, but this dog didn't return. **Thank God.**

I think something clicked in my dad while the music was on. I am sure he was listening to Stevie Wonder, likely dancing to **"Very Superstitious"** on repeat.

We memorized every song he played, not because we liked them but because we rewound the track so much that we could sing it without the player.

It was part of his act, or was it? Same outline, just a different day of the week, and more problematic outrage at times to slaughter my mom. When my father danced, he demanded that everyone pay attention to him. If we didn't obey and love his moves, he would scream, and whoever was out of order quickly straightened up as instructed, or else mom's beating was worse, and it was always her fault, as he said.

An example of us not paying attention to him was an all-nighter. If we had the nerve to close our eyes because we were tired, that was entirely out of the question. His dance was more important than the rest that his children needed. He snatched the doggy from us in the middle of our taking turns to hold our new canine. He put the dog on the ground and told that frightened fragile pup, **"Dance!"**

The Dog Doesn't Dance

Here we go. The puppy ran toward us for protection.
It wasn't my dad. He dared us to touch or help within 5 minutes
of having a new pet.

At this point, I am unsure what to call him. I am referring to my
father.

For this one, I'd say the horrific dog catcher who doesn't care
about any person or animal. Momma should have never said,
"Carroll leave the dog alone."

Daddy quickly responded, " I'm warning you, Bertha, don't test me;
stay out of this!" Tonight my mother will get to share her fight.

The dog will not dance; it's now shivering and barking at him. The
small dog will take some of the anger from the torture my mom
would endure.

Hit one. He told this unnamed dog, "Don't bark! Shut up!"

Terrified, we are shushing the dog. He yelled at us. He said, "Stay
out of it!"

Then he angrily looked at the dog and said, "He will do what I tell
him to do! **Now dance!**"

So my father was such an incredible dancer. When he danced, we could catch a short break from crying and dry our tears, and I am sure we all hoped the violence would end, but it didn't.

My father, blazing mad at this point, does his dance moves as we all watch and then tells the dog, "Your turn." The dog can't remember the exact movements, I assume, because the dog didn't move. **The pup barked.** A more brutal slap for the dog hit two. "Don't you bark at me," in a deep, threatening voice. The little dog slid from the hard lick of his hand.

Running away from an animal ... I know these are the thoughts of the baby pup as my dad caught it.

Bam! Bam! Bam! Bam! Hit three and beyond at this point.

Four licks to the back, he's beating the tiny dog while squeezing him almost to death in his hand. I can't tell if the dog is crying. There is no more barking; it's hurt. All of the children are all crying now, my mother as well.

I said, "Daddy, leave our dog alone; you are hurting him!" Why did I yell that? I got a lecture; he's screaming in my face. He was screeching, "Who bought the dog home?" Daddy reminds me that he would fix me if I didn't mind my tongue.

The Dog Doesn't Dance

What? Does he understand how hard it was for me not to interfere? At this age, I'm a chatterbox. Curious Cassandra, inquisitive all day. The dog limped away from my dad's spot, telling him to stay. Why did our little pet do that?

My dad's thumping hits the dog's back, and it seems like the dog is losing his tiny breath. Slammed on the spot; "Stay, I said! Move again, and I will kill you!" is what my dad said. "But, Dad, I thought you wanted the dog to dance. Maybe the dog wants to show you his moves instead."

My father finalized the death of this precious puppy, literally. The baby pup had no idea he meant those words.

"One more time, you will do what I say," my dad is talking. He shows the dog his moves again. Significantly hurt, the dog didn't move. Picture a new dog rolling on your living room floor, hit by your father's shoe with **brute** force. Significantly hurt, the dog didn't move.

At that moment, I think I felt it; I sure gasped. "Daddy! Please, leave our dog alone!" Yep, that's my motor mouth crying and shouting at him.

"Mind your tongue, little girl! You are going to get it!" And I was. I had no idea what my dad had in store for me. As drunk as he was, he kept his word. I'll share more in my next volume. **Keep following.**

Everyone in the house was crying now. My mother said, **"Cassandra, hush!"** I can't remember if she received a hit from responding; usually, she did.

Focused on what he will do next to our brand new pet, it's only been 30 minutes; honestly, it's less than that. It all occurred in what seemed to be a blink. Yes, this happened quickly. The canine didn't dance. This pooch is exhausted. I don't know what type of wheezing or weeping it's doing, but we are crying waterfalls now.

My brother attempts to speak some sense to my beast of a father. This dog doesn't listen, but he will learn tonight. "Daddy, please stop; you are going to kill him!" My dad said, "Yes, I will, because the dog didn't dance."

Imagine a bouncing ball thrown at a wall. Do you see it? Now picture our dog hurled, although the dog didn't ricochet off the wall like a ball. It fell, lifeless, with no movement, and our new pet didn't spring back.

The meanest dog tamer was his name to me now, and many other words to describe him. Can you believe my dad issued more ill treatment like this precious little dog wasn't wounded enough? Because the dog is still breathing, he's choking the dog right in front of us. We cried outpourings after that.

The Dog Doesn't Dance

Imagine a pet you received as promised, killed by your father because it didn't dance in a half hour? I can't get the picture out of my head. That one is chiseled in forever, I believe.

We got fussed about loving a dog more than our daddy that night.

Yep, my monstrous parent was distraught with all of us. We were so disturbed, unable to show care at that moment. I think we all had swollen eyes that night, unable to see. **Unbearable.**

Our puffy eyelids were caused by crying and looked similar to mom's inflamed eyes from my father hitting her. He wasn't satisfied yet. My dad's rage was still there; you guessed it, mom volunteered. He always said when it was enough. My mom took the other half of the beating, the dog was now dead, and someone had to do it.

After that horrifying instance, my brother wanted another pet. **He asked for a dog a lot.** My mother always denied it. I genuinely believe her response reflected this plagued night. I understand now, and I don't blame her for not allowing it.

⚷━ᴛ Helping heroes thought:

Was he a heartless man, or was he just possessed by dark forces, many ignore or pretend they are not there?

Getting an animal is a big responsibility, not a careless one.

If you are not ready for this obligation, don't become an owner.

Treasure people and pets neither desire to be treated as trash nor beaten to death.

⚷━ᴛ Helping heroes introspection:

These horrific moments endured with my father were traumatic; through my experience, I honestly believe an evil entity possessed him. I refuse to think he was like the tin-man. Even without a heart, the tin-man was civilized and not brutal. And like the tin-man in those dark moments, I am confident he was not operating like those of us, wearing a flesh suit; if he had a heart, it was like a metal of some sort.

⚷━ᴛ You are covenant-created

And I will give them one heart and put a new spirit within them. I will take the heart of stone from them and provide them with a heart of flesh.   Ezekiel 11:19

Moreover, I will give you a new heart and put a new spirit within you, and I will remove the heart of stone from your flesh and give you a heart of flesh. Ezekiel 36:26

To be continued...

Author Contact Page

You may contact the author in the following ways:

Website:
www.DesiredKeysOfTheKing.com

eMail:
cassandra@desiredkeysoftheking.com

www.ingramcontent.com/pod-product-compliance
Lightning Source LLC
Chambersburg PA
CBHW021147020426
42331CB00005B/932